GO FACTS SEASONS
Autumn

A & C BLACK • LONDON

Autumn

First published 2003 in Australia by Blake Education Pty Ltd

This edition published 2005 in the United Kingdom by
A & C Black Publishers Ltd, 37 Soho Square, London W1D 3QZ
www.acblack.com

ISBN-10: 0-7136-7269-2
ISBN-13: 978-0-7136-7269-5

A CIP record for this book is available from the British Library.

Written by Katy Pike
Design and layout by The Modern Art Production Group
Photos by John Foxx, Photodisc, Corel, Brand X, Corbis, Digital Stock,
Image DJ, Rubberball, Image Source, Comstock and Eyewire.

UK series consultant: Julie Garnett

Printed in China by WKT Company Ltd.

A & C Black uses paper produced with elemental chlorine-free pulp,
harvested from managed sustainable forests.

Contents

Signs of Autumn

As summer turns to autumn, what changes can you see and feel?

Autumn days are shorter and cooler. Some days can be windy and cold. The leaves on the trees change colour.

Autumn is the **harvest** season. Farmers harvest crops such as potatoes, apples and pumpkins.

Children are busy at school.

Apples

Hay is harvested in autumn. Some animals eat hay all year long.

DID YOU KNOW?
There are two days a year that day and night are equal length – 12 hours long. One is the autumn equinox on September 22nd or 23rd.

Plants in Autumn

Plants are getting ready for winter.

Deciduous trees lose their leaves. First the leaves change colour. Green leaves change to yellow, orange, red or brown. Then the leaves fall.

Some plants die after dropping their seeds. Many others only look like they are dead. The bulbs and roots of these plants are still alive underground.

Oak leaves and acorns

6

Where have you seen deciduous trees?

Oak trees are deciduous.

7

In the Garden

Many plants drop their seeds in autumn.

Annual plants live for just one year. These plants grow, drop their seeds and then die. Their seeds may grow into new plants next year.

Many vegetables are annual plants. Carrots, pumpkins, lettuce and onions are all annuals.

Squash

8

Pumpkin vines die, leaving the pumpkins sitting on the dirt.

These seeds are ready to fall.

LARGEST!
The largest pumpkin ever grown weighed 572·5 kg.

Raking leaves is an autumn chore for some people.

9

Autumn Food

Pumpkins and apples are autumn foods.

In autumn many vegetables, such as pumpkins and carrots, are sweet and ready to eat. Some kinds of mushrooms grow in forests and fields.

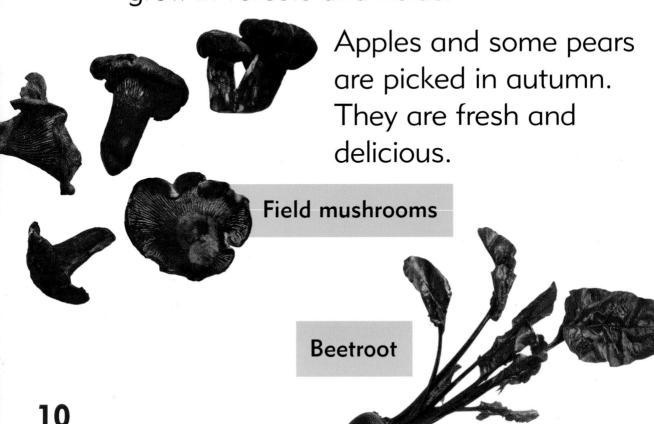

Apples and some pears are picked in autumn. They are fresh and delicious.

Field mushrooms

Beetroot

Apple pies can be eaten hot or cold.

Freshly picked carrots can be steamed or cooked in soups.

Pears can be eaten raw, or baked for dessert.

11

People in Autumn

People spend more time indoors in autumn.

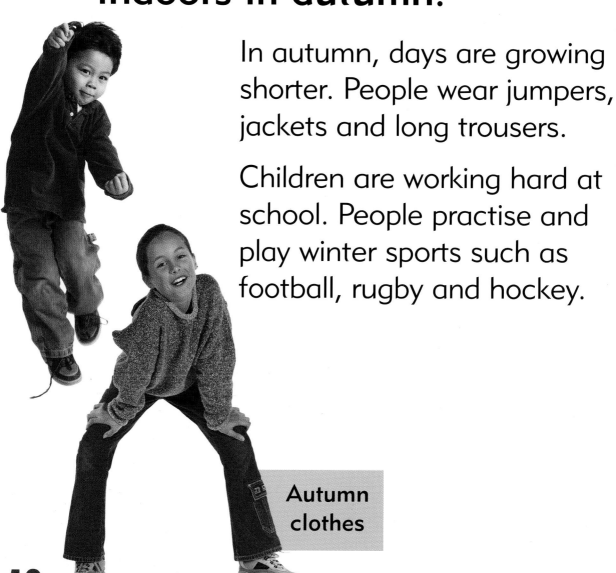

In autumn, days are growing shorter. People wear jumpers, jackets and long trousers.

Children are working hard at school. People practise and play winter sports such as football, rugby and hockey.

Autumn clothes

12

Where did these leaves come from?

Friends get together to play rugby.

Many children play soccer at the weekend.

13

Animals in Autumn

Animals need to prepare for the coming winter.

Some animals, such as dogs and horses, grow thicker fur. Flocks of **migrating** birds fly away. They will spend the winter in a warmer place. In spring they will return to their summer home.

Some countries have warm winters. In these places, animals may still **breed** in autumn.

Duck

14

Some herons migrate to France, Spain or Portugal.

Hedgehogs build a nest out of leaves and grass in autumn.

Migrating birds fly south to warmer places.

Glossary

annual	living for one year
autumn	the season between summer and winter
breed	to have babies
bulb	round shaped root of a plant
crops	plants grown for food
deciduous	loses leaves in autumn
harvest	pick and gather a crop
migrate	move from one place to another

Index

16